PATHS *to* FREEDOM

Daniel Schulman

◀ Harriet Tubman leads runaway slaves to freedom.

Contents

CONSULTANT AND REVIEWER
Sam Goldberger, emeritus professor, Capital Community College, Hartford, Connecticut

BOOK DESIGN/PHOTO RESEARCH
Steve Curtis Design, Inc.

Published by the National Geographic Society
1145 17th Street N.W.
Washington, D.C. 20036-4688

ISBN: 9780792254515

2016
3 4 5 6 7 8 9 10 11 12 13 14 15

Printed in the U.S.A

▲ **People who are free can say what they think.**

What Is Freedom?

Freedom is being able to make your own choices. It means you can say and do what you think is true.

Freedom gives people certain **rights**. People who are free have these rights.

- They can say what they believe.
- They can choose the kind of work they do.
- They can choose a religion.
- They can vote for leaders.

....

freedom – the power to say, do, or think as you please

right – something that is due a person

▲ **People who are free can choose their religion.**

4

▲ People who are free can choose
the kind of work they do.

▲ People who are free can vote
for the leaders they want.

5

Seeking Freed[om]

Big Idea
People often struggle for freedom.

Set Purpose
Read to find out what people do when they are not free.

Many people live in places where they do not have freedom. They cannot make their own choices. They cannot say what they think. They cannot choose what kind of work they do.

Throughout history, people have searched for freedom. People find freedom in different ways. Some people move for freedom. Others work for freedom at home.

Questions You Will Explore

Why do people want freedom?

How do people seek freedom?

om

▶ The Statue of
Liberty is a symbol
of freedom in the
United States.

A Plan for Freedom

The people who **founded** the United States more
than 200 years ago knew that freedom was
important. They wrote on paper their ideas for
a free country. This paper is the **Constitution.**
It explains how the government should work.
Part of the Constitution is the **Bill of Rights.**
It lists freedoms that all Americans share.

People who have freedom also have **responsibilities.**
One responsibility is knowing that others have
rights, too. We should not hurt others or break
the law. But we are free to make choices.

....

found – to start or set up

Constitution – the document that tells how the United States
government should work

Bill of Rights – the part of the Constitution that lists freedoms

responsibility – something that people should do

▼ **The Constitution**

8

Freedom of Speech

People can say what they think, without fear. This means people can disagree with one another or the government about what should be done.

Freedom of the Press

News reporters can tell the news as they see it. This helps people understand events and make their own opinions.

Freedom of Religion

People can choose their religion. In free countries, there are often many different religions.

Seeking Freedom

Some countries do not have laws that protect people's freedoms. What do people in those countries do to find freedom?

Sometimes people leave their homes. They might move to a country with more freedom. This can be very hard, though. People who move to a new country might have to learn a new language and way of life.

England

Cuba

People Who Have Moved for Freedom

English, 1600s
The Pilgrims began to leave for the Americas in 1620. They left England because they were not allowed to practice their religion.

Germans, 1930s
Many Germans, especially Jews, left Germany because of a cruel government. They moved to other countries to find freedom.

Reasons to Leave Home

Millions of people have left their homes in search of freedom. Often they want freedom to practice their religion. They want the freedom to pick their leaders. People move for freedom of speech and freedom of the press. People also move because they want a better education or jobs.

Germany

Vietnam

Cubans, 1960s

Many Cubans left their island country in the 1960s. They left because their government did not allow them to pick their leaders.

Vietnamese, 1970s

Many people from Vietnam left to escape war. People there were also not free to speak out or to choose their work.

Working for Freedom at Home

People do not always move for freedom. Sometimes they struggle for it at home. That happened in South Africa. About 20 years ago, South Africa had a system called **apartheid.** Apartheid means "separation." Apartheid was a set of unfair laws. These laws took away freedoms for some people because of the color of their skin.

Nelson Mandela fought against apartheid. He was even jailed for speaking out. But he won! Apartheid laws were changed. Like many others, Mandela thought freedom was worth fighting for.

....

apartheid – a set of unfair laws that kept black people from having the same freedoms as white people

AFRICA

South Africa

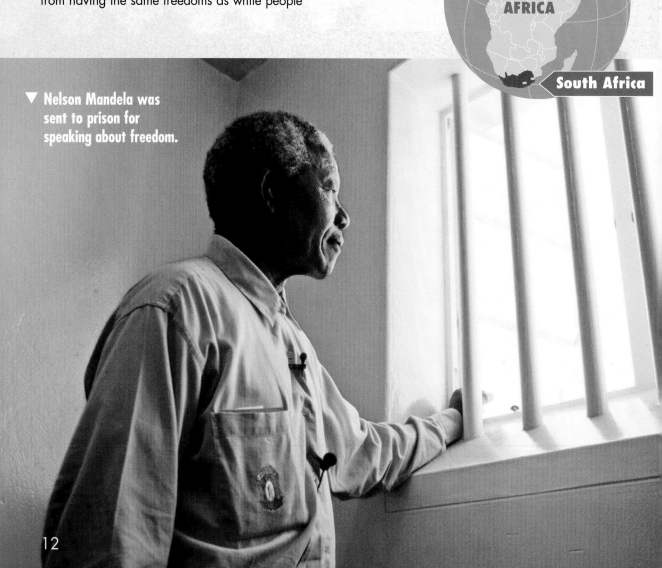

▼ Nelson Mandela was sent to prison for speaking about freedom.

Students Speak Out

In 1989, thousands of Chinese students gathered. They met in Tiananmen Square in Beijing, China. They were there to peacefully **protest** unfair laws. They wanted more freedom from their government.

The students did not succeed. China's government sent in the army to stop the students. Hundreds of students were killed. People in China still do not have many freedoms.

....

protest – to speak out against

ASIA

China

▼ **Students in Tiananmen Square carried signs asking for fair laws.**

The Right to Vote

People in the United States have struggled for the freedom we have now. For many years women could not vote. They did not have the same rights as men.

Women who wanted to vote began to join together. They held meetings and protests. Some were even arrested and jailed. On August 26, 1920, women in the United States finally gained the right to vote. Today, women still struggle for equality in many ways.

▼ Dr. Martin Luther King, Jr. protested unfair treatment of African Americans.

▼ Women marched and protested to gain the right to vote.

Freedom for All

African Americans in the United States did not always have the same freedoms as other Americans. Many were kept from voting. Some were not allowed to go to good schools. Others were not allowed to use or enjoy the same things as white people.

In the 1960s, people protested. They said African Americans should have the same rights as all Americans. These protests helped change the laws.

Stop and Think!

HOW do people seek freedom?

15

Recap
Name some ways that people seek freedom.

Set Purpose
Read to learn about brave Americans seeking freedom.

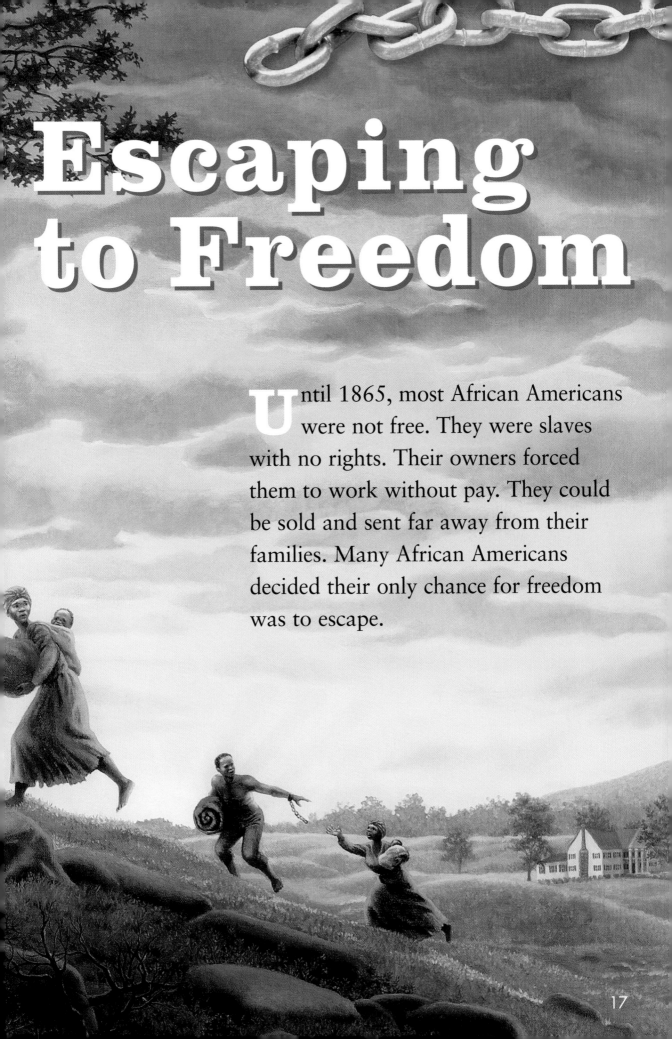

Escaping to Freedom

Until 1865, most African Americans were not free. They were slaves with no rights. Their owners forced them to work without pay. They could be sold and sent far away from their families. Many African Americans decided their only chance for freedom was to escape.

Bonds of Slavery

In 1830, Josiah Henson was 41 years old. A life of slavery was all he had ever known. Born in Maryland, Henson was taken from his family as a child. He was bought and sold many times.

Henson lived on a **plantation,** or large farm, in Kentucky. He had a wife and four children. He tried to buy his way out of slavery. But his owner, Amos Riley, tricked him. He kept the money that Henson paid for his freedom.

....

plantation – a large farm with many workers

▶ **Josiah Henson in later life**

18

Bad News

One day Henson learned some troubling news. Riley planned to sell him. Henson would have to move to Louisiana. He might never see his wife and children again! Henson could not accept this. So he made a plan for his family to escape.

▲ Many slaves worked on plantations.

▲ This doll was a slave child's toy.

The Path to Freedom

One dark night, Henson and his family left their home. He carried his two youngest children in a backpack. The family boarded a small boat. They crossed the Ohio River into Indiana.

Once in Indiana, the family had to move slowly. They had to be careful not to be seen. Some slave owners offered rewards for the capture of escaped slaves. If the family was found, they might be returned to Riley. Henson's family often traveled at night and slept during the day.

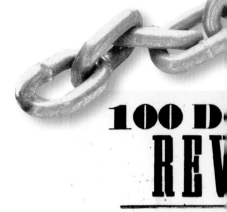

100 D
REV

Ranaway from the
ly, my Black Woman

EM

Seventeen years of a
has a whining voice.
calico and one blue a
ed gingham bonnet; a
pers. I will pay the
the Ohio river on the
HUNDRED DOLLA
Ohio, and delivered t
County, Ky.
August 4, 1853.

▼ People helped escaped slaves
on the path to freedom.

Free at Last

The family traveled to Canada by wagon, by boat, and on foot. Slavery was not allowed in Canada. Along the way, people helped the family. Some gave them food. Others hid them in barns.

The family set foot in Canada more than a month after their daring escape. Henson's first words were, "I am free!"

◀ Some slave owners offered rewards for the capture of runaway slaves.

▲ People hid escaped slaves in wagons and other secret places.

Freedom Train

How was Henson's family able to make the trip to freedom? They went on something called the Underground Railroad. But it did not have train cars or tracks. It did not go underground. It was made of people who helped slaves run away.

People along the Underground Railroad gave runaways food to eat. They gave runaways a place to stay. They carried runaways closer to freedom in boats or wagons.

Paths to Freedom

■ Free States
■ Slave States
↑ Underground Railroad

Secret Paths to Freedom

The Underground Railroad was secret. We do not know all the paths people traveled. But we do know that the Underground Railroad helped many slaves escape to freedom. Some journeys took a month. Others took a year or more. Some runaways were captured or died along the way. The Underground Railroad shows how far people will go for freedom.

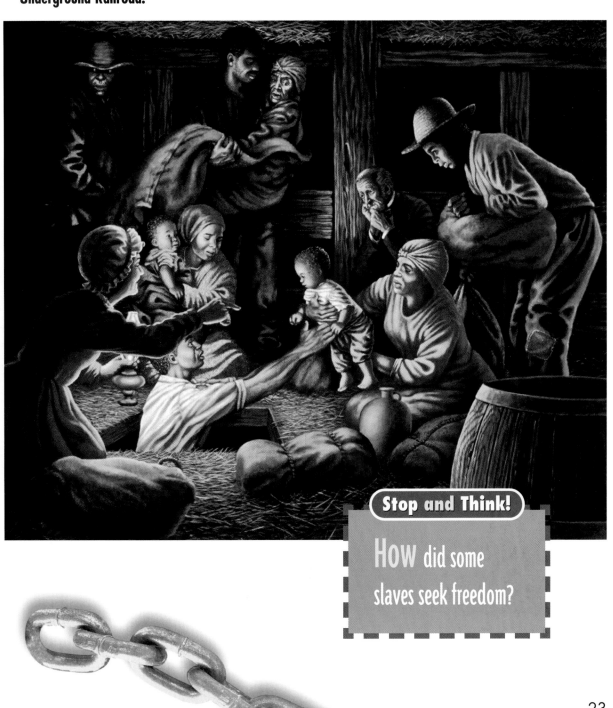

▼ Many people helped slaves along the Underground Railroad.

Stop and Think!

HOW did some slaves seek freedom?

Recap
Explain why people seek freedom.

Set Purpose
Read to learn more about seeking freedom.

CONNECT WHAT YOU HAVE LEARNED

Paths to Freedom

Most people want freedom. They want to decide what they can say, write, and believe.

Here are some ideas that you learned about freedom.

- Freedom gives people rights and responsibilities.
- Laws protect people's freedoms in some countries.
- Some people move in search of freedom.
- Some people speak out or fight to try to gain freedom.

Check What You Have Learned

Why do people want freedom?

▲ Freedom gives people the right to say what they think.

▲ The Constitution guarantees certain freedoms in the United States.

▲ Many Cubans move to the United States for freedom.

▲ People in China protest to gain freedom.

▲ Dr. Martin Luther King, Jr. wanted all citizens to vote for their leaders.

The Right to Vote

It has not been easy to make sure that everyone in the United States is treated fairly. Even 100 years after gaining freedom from slavery, African Americans still struggled for equal rights.

In some states it was difficult for African Americans to vote. Some were forced to pay a tax they could not afford in order to vote. Finally, in the 1960s, new laws were made. These laws made sure all adult citizens could vote without having to pay.

26

A Living Document

The Constitution is often called a "living document." This means that it can change as the needs of the country change. The Constitution has had 27 amendments, or changes.

The amendments shown in the chart gave more people the right to vote. These changes have helped the government make sure that all adults have rights and freedoms.

▶ Women marched and protested to gain the right to vote.

SOME CONSTITUTIONAL AMENDMENTS

AMENDMENT	YEAR APPROVED	CHANGE TO THE CONSTITUTION
19th	1920	Women gain the right to vote.
24th	1964	Voting taxes are banned.
26th	1971	Citizens can vote starting at age 18.

The Search for Freedom Continues

Freedom is spreading around the world. But there are still many places where people are not free. They cannot practice their religion. They cannot take part in government. They cannot say openly what they think.

Until recently, people in Afghanistan had very few freedoms. Women were not allowed to go to school or work. They could not be seen in public. Men were punished or killed if they did not follow the government's rules.

Countries around the world helped the people of Afghanistan. Now those people have important rights. They have a new constitution. It says that citizens have the right to vote. They can choose who will stand up and speak for them. The new constitution says that girls can go to school. It also says that women can work and move freely in public.

▶ Girls in Afghanistan now have the right to go to school.

◄ Men and women
prepare for law
school in Afghanistan.

Many kinds of words are used in this book. Here you will learn about compound words and words that have more than one meaning.

Compound Words

A compound word is made by joining two shorter words. You can often figure out what a compound word means by knowing what the two shorter words mean.

under + ground = underground

Subways are trains that travel **underground.**

run + away = runaway

People who escape are called **runaways.**

Multiple-Meaning Words

Some words have more than one meaning. Think about the two meanings for each of these words. Then use each word in a sentence of your own.

She has a **right** to vote.

He raised his **right** hand.

Many people worked hard to **found** the United States.

He **found** a nickel on the sidewalk.

Press the button on the elevator.

The **press** reports the news each day.

Research and Write

Write About Freedom

Choose a person from history who has fought for freedom. For example, you could choose Nelson Mandela or Dr. Martin Luther King, Jr. Research how they reached those freedoms. Did they protest? Did they march? Then write an informational report.

Research

Collect books and reference materials, or go online.

Read and Take Notes

As you read, take notes and draw pictures.

Write

Then write about how the person you chose achieved the goal of freedom.

▶ **Nelson Mandela**

Read and Compare

Read More About Freedom

Find and read other books about freedom. As you read, think about these questions.

- What kind of freedoms do people fight for?
- What kind of freedoms do you have?
- How would life be different without those freedoms?

Books to Read

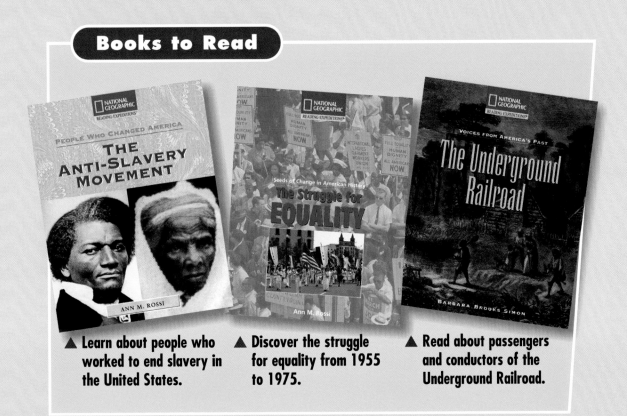

▲ Learn about people who worked to end slavery in the United States.

▲ Discover the struggle for equality from 1955 to 1975.

▲ Read about passengers and conductors of the Underground Railroad.

Glossary

apartheid (page 12)
A set of unfair laws that kept black people from having the same freedoms as white people
Apartheid kept black people from having rights in South Africa.

Bill of Rights (page 8)
The part of the Constitution that lists freedoms
The Bill of Rights protects the freedom of the press.

Constitution (page 8)
The document that tells how the United States government should work
The Constitution is a written plan for the United States government.

found (page 8)
To start or set up
The United States was founded more than 200 years ago.

freedom (page 4)
The power to say, do, or think as you please
Freedom is being able to say what you think.

KEY CONCEPT

plantation (page 18)
A large farm with many workers
Josiah Henson lived on a plantation in Kentucky.

protest (page 13)
To speak out against
People often protest unfair treatment.

responsibility (page 8)
Something that people should do
People have a responsibility to speak out against unfair laws.

right (page 4)
Something that is due a person
Americans have the right to choose their leaders.

Index